IMAGES
of England

SHAFTESBURY

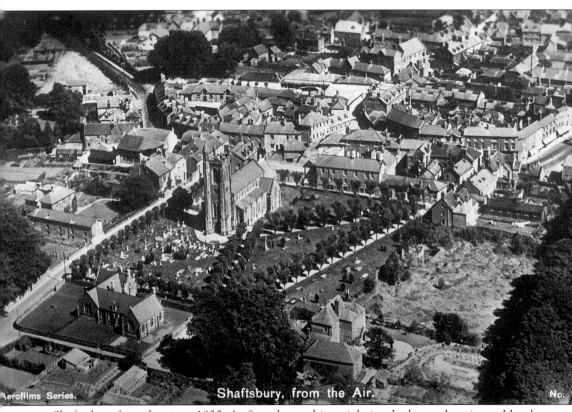

Shaftsbury, from the Air.

Shaftesbury from the air, *c.* 1930. At first glance this aerial view looks much as it would today, but closer inspection it reveals many changes. To the front left of the scene is the Town Primary School, which has been converted into private flats. Note the absence of houses in front of the school on the corner of Abbey Walk. Behind the school is Holy Trinity church, which was then the town's main place of worship. To the right of the triangle of trees in Holy Trinity are the Abbey Ruins, in a very overgrown state. Behind the church is a tight cluster of houses, which are nowadays long gone and have been replaced with a car park and supermarket. To the left of Holy Trinity is a row of buildings, erected before the construction of the (now demolished) Savoy cinema. This view is an ideal way to start this collection of photographs that will show some of the changes in the Shaftesbury landscape over the past 100 years.

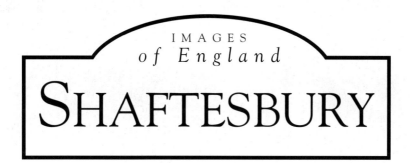

IMAGES
of England

SHAFTESBURY

Compiled by
Eric Olsen

TEMPUS

First published 1998
Copyright © Eric Olsen, 1998

Tempus Publishing Limited
The Mill, Brimscombe Port,
Stroud, Gloucestershire, GL5 2QG

ISBN 0 7524 1157 8

Typesetting and origination by
Tempus Publishing Limited
Printed in Great Britain by
Midway Clark Printing, Wiltshire

This book is dedicated to my mother and father,
Edna Olsen and Edwin Olsen,
who both loved Shaftesbury

Contents

Acknowledgements

I am grateful to all the local people who have lent me photographs of Shaftesbury and to those who have shared personal memories with me – without their help, the compilation of this book would not have been possible. I would especially like to thank Mr Witcher for the loan of many fascinating photographs and Mr and Mrs Padfield for supplying me with names and information on some of the more intriguing images. Thanks must also go to Shaftesbury's prominent photographers over the years, including Mr Tyler and A.J. Bealing.

Introduction

Several photographs of Shaftesbury, taken by my father Edwin Olsen in the 1940s and 1950s, were passed down to me after his death in 1956. Over the years, I studied this fascinating series and noticed the gradual change in the scenery and buildings. This led me to gather other photographs of the town and I have amassed a large collection, which dates back to the turn of the century. Shaftesbury was my birthplace and home for twenty years and, although I no longer live there, I am still regularly drawn to visit this charming and picturesque town. I felt it only right to share this collection of photographs and this book has been compiled with that aim very much in mind.

Thomas Hardy, Dorset's most famous novelist, described Shaftesbury as 'A city of a dream'. This is borne out with the disappearance over the centuries of its great medieval Abbey, twelve churches and three mints. The greatest asset of the modern town is its marvellous views over the vales, both from Castle Hill and Park Walk and, of course, Gold Hill – one of the most photographed streets in England.

Shaftesbury is a thriving market town standing on a greensand spur overlooking the Blackmore Vale. It is over 700 feet above sea level. From Neolithic times, man probably used the site for observation and defence, but there is no evidence of a permanent settlement. This is probably due to the lack of water because of its high position. Tradition claims that a town called Caer Palladwr flourished on this site. The town has received a variety of names from historians, who record it as: Sceptonia, Schefton, Sceptesberie, Sceapterbyrig or Sceaftesbyrig. The two latter names came from the Saxon words 'sceap', meaning promontory, and 'byrig', meaning fortified settlement. Because of its connection with King Edward, it was also known as Edwardstowe for a short time. A house in Bimport still bears this name. The most recent name, Shaston, was popularised by Thomas Hardy.

The first defended settlement probably stood around Castle Hill and the western end of Bimport, because of the natural defence of the fall of the hill on three sides. A palisaded earth embankment protected the last side up Stoney Lane and across Bimport. Because of its extensive view and natural defences, it was here in 880 AD that King Alfred rebuilt the town and founded the Abbey. He placed the Abbey to the east of the original settlement with a wall, which ran from the top of Gold Hill to the top of Tout Hill. A gate was placed across Bimport. The name Bimport, or 'Binan Port', roughly translated, means 'a road within a gate'. In the thirteenth century, the Abbey walls were extended down the hillside to St James, thus enclosing the park. The massive buttressed wall down Gold Hill is the remains of the Abbey wall. The Abbey had considerable royal connections. Alfred the Great's grandson, Athelstan, authorised three royal mints in Shaftesbury, which struck a series of silver pennies bearing the town name. The coins were of such good quality that, after the conquest, the Normans adopted them instead of producing their own. In the nineteenth century, Hudson and Co struck the first coin to the value of threepence (a silver threepenny bit) in Shaftesbury.

One of the most momentous events in the town's history occurred on 20 February 979, when King Edward was buried in the Abbey after his murder at Corfe Castle. Following his tragic death, he was considered a martyr and pilgrims came to pray at his tomb, where miraculous cures occurred. He was canonised 'St Edward King and Martyr' because of this, possibly on 20 June 1001 as this is his saint's day. King Canute was converted to Christianity and took a great interest in Shaftesbury and its Abbey and indeed this was where he died on 12 November 1035. He was buried at Winchester. In 1392, Richard II confirmed the grant of two markets to Shaftesbury, one on a Monday and one on a Saturday, as well as Sunday during August. Fairs were also held at certain times of the year. At the dissolution of the monasteries, on 23 May 1539, the last Abbess, Elizabeth Zouche, surrendered the Abbey to the King's commissioner, Sir John Tregwell. Six hundred years of history were wiped out as the Abbey church and other buildings were demolished and the lands sold. Much of the stone from the Abbey was plundered and used to build houses around Shaftesbury. The Abbey site was purchased by Sir Thomas Arundel and then passed through various hands, including those of the Earl of Pembroke and the Grosvenors.

The town suffered a decline over the next couple of centuries. However, the eighteenth century saw a revival. Five turnpike roads converged on Shaftesbury, the main one being the turnpike from Salisbury to Exeter, the others to Bristol, Bath and Poole. Coaches would come to rest in the courtyard of the Grosvenor Hotel, which was then called the Red Lion. Lord Grosvenor bought a large part of the town in the early nineteenth century and spent liberally on improving dwellings and civic projects, including the Town Hall and the Market Hall. The cattle market was revived in 1902.

The 'Sale of Shaftesbury' in 1919 was another of the town's great events. Lord Stalbridge owned a major part of the town and sold it as a job lot to a syndicate of three local businessmen. They, in turn, resold it by public auction over three days in the Market Hall in May 1919. This led to shopkeepers and householders owning their own properties instead of renting them from the Lords of the Manor, as had been the case for centuries. In the years since the sale in 1919, Shaftesbury has prospered and grown eastwards. New suburbs, schools, an industrial estate, a bypass, and a new health centre have sprung up. Fortunately, the town centre has so far escaped any out-of-character modernisation and still retains its, mainly Victorian, charm. Let us hope this will be the case for many years to come.

One

The Town Centre

St Peter's church, c. 1900. This is the oldest surviving church in Shaftesbury. In mediaeval times, Shaftesbury boasted twelve churches. St Peter's dates from the thirteenth century, but there is evidence of an even earlier building on this site. During the 1970s, the church was restored and replaced Holy Trinity as the main parish church of Shaftesbury. A service of rededication was held on 30 September 1977.

The Commons, c. 1900. The house next to the Town Hall was demolished to make way for a garage, following the advent of the motor car.

The Commons, c. 1900. An omnibus stands outside the Grosvenor Hotel. This was used to carry guests to and from Semley station. On the opposite side of the road a group of postal workers are stood outside the post office, including one on a horse and cart. The occupants of the flat above the post office are sitting on the window ledge so as to be included in the photograph.

10

The Commons, c. 1900. Next to the Grosvenor Hotel is Harry Imber's butchers shop. To the front is George Elsey's confectioners. Above the shop was the Cosy Corner restaurant. A note from a trade directory of the time reveals that 'George Elsey was a steam biscuit manufacturer and confectioner. Manufacturer of fruit syrups, limejuice and British cordials'. He also patented the Crown Machine for making and kneading dough.

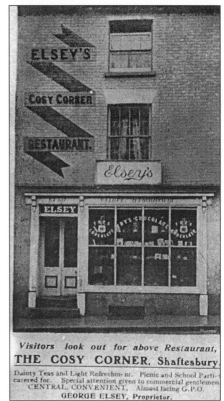

Advertisement from a town guide, c. 1905.

The Commons, *c.* 1910. Around the lamp-post in the centre of the Commons is an array of machinery. Therefore this photograph must have been taken on a Saturday, which was market day, for it was then that Farris' Belle Vue Ironworks, which was on the corner of Victoria Street, used to display and sell agricultural machinery . 'Chadder' Hall, who lived in Salisbury Street, would also have a selection of lawnmowers, which he had bought in and refurbished, for sale.

The Commons, *c.* 1925. Motor cars and motorcycles have now taken the place of the horse and cart. In the centre of the Commons is the National Provincial Bank. During the years after the First World War, this was also the labour exchange. It was not unusual to see a queue of up to 100 men outside this building due to the lack of work at this time.

The Commons, *c.* 1930. The post office has now been moved to a building near the Kings Arms public house and its former site taken over by the Midland Bank. Next to the bank is the Butt of Sherry, wine merchants. Pike and Badger's garage can be seen next to the Town Hall: this was originally Hill and Boll Motor Works and had been taken over in 1913.

The Commons, *c.* 1950. J. W. Pearsons' stationers business has expanded and, by this time, he has his own printing works, above his shop, called the Abbey Press.

The Commons, *c.* 1960. The garage next to the Town Hall is now V.F. Pike and Co. Ltd. This building was totally out of character with its surroundings. If put before a planning committee today, a building like this would surely be turned down immediately.

The Commons, *c.* 1930. The archway between the pillars of the Grosvenor Hotel leads into the courtyard of this old coaching inn. Originally this was called the Red Lion: the lane behind the hotel is still called Lions Lane.

The Chevy Chase Sideboard. The Grosvenor Hotel houses this masterpiece of Victorian wood carving by Gerald Robinson. This intricately carved solid oak sideboard is twelve feet long and ten feet high and depicts the battle of Chevy Chase in 1388.

King Alfred's Kitchen, c. 1930. The front of this building has hardly altered over the last hundred years. It has not always been a cafe and was once a private house. Parts of the building date back to the thirteenth century.

Pencil illustration of the Market Hall, drawn at the end of the eighteenth century. Shaftesbury was a thriving market town in the sixteenth century and Edmund Bower, mayor of the town in 1550, built the Market Hall in the roadway alongside St Peter's church, to give shelter to the market people and their wares. The top of the building was used for council meetings. The area by St Peter's was known as the Cornmarket. Sheep were penned in between the buttresses on Gold Hill and cattle were grazed on the Park. A covered market stood in the centre of the Commons for the sale of butter, cheese and poultry. The fish market stood on the site of the present Town Hall. The Market Hall stood for nearly 300 years, before being demolished in 1820 to widen the road in order to facilitate the passage of carts and carriages.

St Peter's church, *c.* 1930. The crypt of the church was originally the cellar of the Sun and Moon Inn, next door, which is now a private house. The fireplace where the ale was brewed can still be seen today. The cellar was sold to the church in 1907 for £50.

King Alfred's Kitchen, *c.* 1950. Car parking outside the Town Hall became a problem after the war. Jack Padfield, a former harness maker, was given the unofficial job of car park attendant and made a living out of ensuring cars were parked correctly for tips of a penny or twopence a time. He later went on to be the Town Hall caretaker until he retired.

Town Hall, *c.* 1900. The Town Hall was built in 1826 to replace the Market Hall. The wooden clock tower was added in 1879. The slower and simpler pace of life at the beginning of the twentieth century is typified in this scene. The children are playing with a hoop, a popular toy at this time.

High Street, *c.* 1900. This seems a very peaceful Victorian afternoon. It is interesting to note that the shop on the left, Strange and Sons, a bootmakers and leather sellers, is trying to increase business and has sale posters in the window.

High Street, *c.* 1900. This shows how rare a spectacle photographers were at this time. The whole of the High Street has come to a standstill to pose for this photograph.

Town Hall, *c.* 1925. A sunny, late-afternoon scene outside the Town Hall. Horse-drawn carts share the road with cars. An indication that the roads have got busier since the previous pictures is a 'Keep to the left' sign fixed to the lamp-post in the middle of the road.

St Peter's church and High Street, 1923. Note the absence of the Town Hall clock. This picture was taken in the interval between the wooden tower being taken down and the new stone clock tower being erected. On the left is the original Mitre Inn building which was built close to the east wall of St Peter's. This was pulled down in 1933 and rebuilt a little further east.

20

Town Hall, *c.* 1940. The recently rebuilt Mitre Inn can be seen on the left, with its new entrance door by St Peter's church.

Town Hall, *c.* 1940. Another two signs have appeared on the lamp-post in the centre of the road: one to indicate the presence of public telephones and one for the recently built public conveniences either side of the Town Hall.

Town Hall, *c.* 1970. The author himself is in this scene, standing in the grammar school uniform, second from the right. Eddie Prowse, the author's brother-in-law – then manager of W.H. Smith and Sons – is crossing the road.

Town Hall, *c.* 1960. The Town Hall, complete with three Christmas trees, just before Christmas, covered with a light sprinkling of snow. To the left of the door is a nativity scene.

SHAFTESBURY - - DORSET

2¼ miles from Semley Station (L. & S.W. Rly.); 8 from Sturminster Newton; 12 from Blandford, and on the main road from London to Exeter, being about 102 miles from London

ILLUSTRATED PARTICULARS WITH PLANS

OF THE MAJOR PORTION OF

THE TOWN OF SHAFTESBURY

WELL KNOWN AS AN INLAND HEALTH RESORT

Comprising about FIFTY SHOPS WITH DWELLING HOUSES NATIONAL PROVINCIAL BANK AND LLOYDS 'BANK 250 HOUSES AND COTTAGES, INCLUDING EIGHT VERY ATTRACTIVE & FIRST-CLASS RESIDENTIAL PROPERTIES GROSVENOR HOUSE SCHOOL, a high-class and well-known School for Girls, comprising excellent premises with modern scholastic buildings and standing in large grounds; CHAPEL; FOUR LICENSED HOUSES MARKET HOUSE AND CATTLE MARKET, ETC., ETC. PLAYING FIELDS, ABOUT 21 ACRES; ALLOTMENTS NUMEROUS FIRST-CLASS BUILDING SITES

ALSO THE VERY VALUABLE AND INTERESTING SITE OF
THE ABBEY EXCAVATIONS

Of special interest to Archæologists and Antiquarians, being the site of the ancient Benedictine Abbey of Shaftesbury, together with

HOLYROOD FARM

in the Parish of Cann, an Important Dairy Holding of about 125 acres with Attractive FARM HOUSE. The whole property produces, at extremely low rentals (excluding properties in hand)

ABOUT £4,446 PER ANNUM

WHICH

MESSRS. FOX & SONS

Are favoured with instructions to Sell by Auction (unless previously disposed of by Private Treaty) in a large number of Lots, at the

MARKET HOUSE, SHAFTESBURY
On Tuesday, Wednesday and Thursday
May 27, 28 and 29, at 11 and 2.30 o'clock
each day precisely

Copies of the Particulars and Conditions of Sale (2/6 each) can be obtained of the Solicitors, MESSRS. BURRIDGE, KENT & FORRESTER, Shaftesbury, at the Grosvenor Arms Hotel, Shaftesbury, or of the Auctioneers, 44 & 48, Old Christchurch Road, Bournemouth, and Branch Offices

Richmond Printeries — Bournemouth —

Notice of Sale, 1919. Lord Stalbridge owned nearly all the properties in the town before 1919. He sold everything together, privately, for the sum of £80,000 to three gentlemen: Dr Harris, Robert Borley and Herbert Vinney. They became known locally as 'the syndicate'. Each of these persons had a specific interest in certain properties in the town and they decided to sell the rest by public auction in May 1919. Most of the shopkeepers and cottagers had rented from Lord Stalbridge and were afraid that, at the proposed public auction, wealthy outsiders would outbid them for their properties. They formed a tenants' association to keep prices down by members promising to bid only for the properties they occupied. In the event, this tactic worked extremely well and emancipated the townspeople as most of them now owned the freehold of their properties.

High Street, *c.* 1900. A busy, sunny day in the High Street. A policeman is riding his bicycle in the centre of the road outside St Peter's church. On the right is Stratton, Sons and Mead, wholesale and retail grocers. This was the largest business in the town at the time. They supplied shops for miles around, even sending local eggs and cheese to retailers in London.

High Street, *c.* 1950. Next to Hine and Parsons, the triangular frontage to the Market Hall can be seen. This used to run from the High Street through to Bell Street. The Bell Street end is now the Arts Centre: at this time it was the sales rooms of John Jeffery and son.

High Street, *c.* 1900. F. W. Young and Sons, the ironmongers, have a marvellous display of goods spilling out onto the pavement. A sign in the shop window shows they also sold guns and ammunition.

High Street, *c.* 1920. To the right is James Hill's tobacconists, with a sign above his shop for Abdulla cigarettes. On the opposite side of the road, a young boy stands outside the Wilts and Dorset Bank.

High Street, *c.* 1935. W. H. Smith and Sons is on the right. It has a sign outside showing that it was a booking office for Black and White coaches.

High Street, *c.* 1910. This was taken from the corner of Mustons Lane looking down to Angel Square. Nos 47 and 49 are the shop of William Henry Baker who, judging from a trade directory of the time, was an earthenware and marine store dealer selling fresh fish. The building on the left, behind the group of people, is the Palace picture house.

High Street, *c*. 1920. A splendid looking car is parked outside the Palace picture house. On the opposite side of the road, a postman is standing outside two private houses, which have since been demolished and replaced with shops.

High Street, *c*. 1920. A group of men stand outside Reg Humphries' bicycle and motorcycle shop. Next door is the grand, pillared front of the Palace. Amidst the group of men, Mr Peach, the barber, has come from his shop across the road to join in the photograph.

High Street, c. 1925. The Palace has now been demolished.

High Street, 1953. The flags hanging across the street reveal that this is Coronation Day, 2 June 1953. Norton's radio and television shop is on the left. The Coronation was one of the first major events to be televised: it must have boosted Mr Norton's business.

Salisbury Street, 1953. A house stands where Anstee's cake shop is today. Next door is Smales the grocer. This was a time when shopping was less stressful than it is in today's self-service supermarkets. You could hand your weekly shopping list to Mr Smales and he would pack your groceries for you and even deliver them straight to your door.

Post office, c. 1950. The building of the post office was started before the Second World War, but not completed until after hostilities had ceased. It was built to replace the smaller premises that were opposite the Ship Inn (now part of the car park).

Angel Square, *c.* 1910. A splendid carnival scene outside Philip Short, coach and carriage builders. This building stands on the modern site of the post office. Just above the sign is a sundial. Mrs Norton, the mayor in 1933, had the foresight to have this saved when the coachworks were pulled down and reinstated it on the wall of the new post office where it remains today. The cart is loaded with sacks of potatoes and vegetables; rabbits and poultry are hanging from the rails. These goods were donated by the townspeople and then sold from the cart. The profits would go to the carnival fund which, in the days before the National Health Service, paid for the running of Shaftesbury's hospital.

Angel Lane, *c.* 1930. Angel Lane took its name from the Angel Inn, which stood on the site of the post office in the seventeenth and eighteenth centuries. When the foundations for the post office were being dug, five wells, which probably used to supply the water for brewing, were found. In those days each inn made its own beer.

Coppice Street, *c.* 1910. Looking down Coppice Street towards Angel Square. This must have been a marvellous way to enter the town. Sadly, all the cottages have long since disappeared. The area today looks totally different, with the few remaining relatively modern houses boarded up, awaiting proposed development. A large tree can be seen behind the shops in the lower end of the High Street.

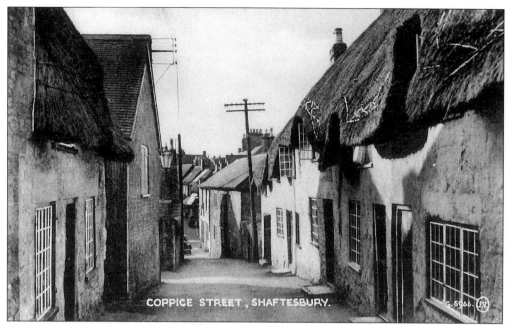

Coppice Street, *c*. 1930. Telegraph poles have started to appear in the streets. The tree in the last photograph has now been felled. Coppice Street took its name from the wood called 'Lone Coppice', which stood on this site.

Coppice Street, *c*. 1930. Mr Hall, the milkman, is pouring milk from a large churn on the back of his cart.

Salisbury Street, *c.* 1920. The men rest from their work, waiting to lift the heavy steel drainage pipes into the trench. The second man from the left is Mr Conduit.

Salisbury Street, *c.* 1900. Fredrick Woodcock, a clockmaker, owned the shop on the left with the blinds. Behind, at no. 6, are the premises of James Burden, the baker and corn factor. The sign above the shop can (just about) still be seen today above the present establishments.

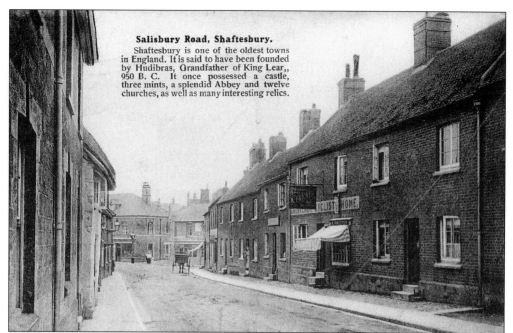

Salisbury Road, Shaftesbury.

Shaftesbury is one of the oldest towns in England. It is said to have been founded by Hudibras, Grandfather of King Lear, 950 B. C. It once possessed a castle, three mints, a splendid Abbey and twelve churches, as well as many interesting relics.

Salisbury Street, c. 1900. On the right is the Grosvenor Coffee Tavern, owned by Alfred Fricker. The sign advertises 'refreshments and rooms with aired beds'. This was also called The Grosvenor Cyclist Home, showing he catered for the aficionados of that popular turn-of-the-century pastime.

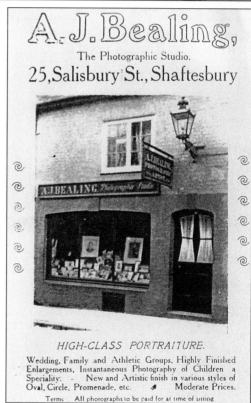

A.J.Bealing,

The Photographic Studio.

25, Salisbury St., Shaftesbury

HIGH-CLASS PORTRAITURE.

Wedding, Family and Athletic Groups, Highly Finished Enlargements, Instantaneous Photography of Children a Speciality. New and Artistic finish in various styles of Oval, Circle, Promenade, etc. Moderate Prices.

Terms All photographs to be paid for at time of sitting

Advertisement, c. 1910. A.J. Bealing was one of Shaftesbury's most popular photographers at the time. This advertisement appeared in the town guide.

Salisbury Street, looking up towards Angel Square, c. 1900. This street has altered little to this day. The people in the scene look reasonably affluent and well-dressed, so this was probably one of the more salubrious areas of the town at this time

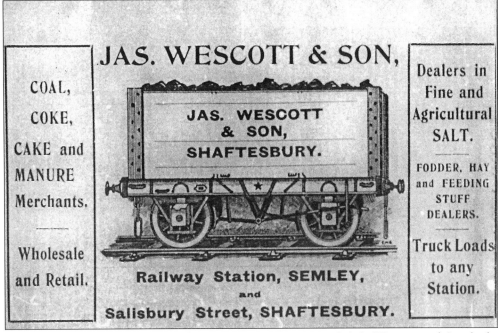

Advertisement from the town guide, c. 1905. For many years, J.A.S. Wescott and Son had a coal yard in Salisbury Street. They also had a yard at Semley Station, where the coal was delivered by train.

St Edward Cafe, *c.* 1950. This cafe and hotel stood almost opposite the Catholic church in Salisbury Street. Behind it is the Knowles Arms public house and, beyond that, the original Spillers almshouse, which was a grand-looking building, built in 1830. Sadly, all three of these buildings have gone and been replaced by St Edwards Court and Spillers House.

St Edward Cafe, *c.* 1950. Through the window, the entrance to St Edwards Catholic church can clearly be seen across the road.

St Edward's Presbytery, *c.* 1930. The presbytery was built in 1923 and is halfway down Great Lane. Boyne Mead path runs behind it. The Roman Catholic church of St Edward, in Salisbury Street just east of the top of Great Lane, was opened in September 1910.

St Rumbold's (or Cann) church, *c.* 1910. The church was rebuilt in 1840 to replace a thirteenth-century building. It ceased to be a parish church in 1971, when it became the grammar school chapel and then, in 1983, the Upper School arts centre. During the early part of this century, the parish boundaries were altered, with the unusual consequence that Cann church was situated outside its own parish.

Two

Park Walk

Park Walk, c. 1910. One of the town's greatest assets is Park Walk and its splendid vistas over the vales. Arguably, no other town in England can boast such magnificent views. Park Walk was created and given to the town in 1753 by Robert Dynley, lord of the manor. A few years later, the trees were planted. The plan was to continue the walk around to Castle Hill, which would have made it one of the finest walks in the country. However, Mr Dynley died before its completion, supposedly from a chill caught supervising the works on the park.

Park Walk, c. 1950. The rows of sycamore trees can be seen running along the entire length of the park. Sadly, in 1955 and 1956, most of these splendid sycamores, which for so long had been a great feature of the park, had to be felled after becoming unsafe due to two violent storms: this provoked much public protest.

Coronation Gardens, Park Walk, 1953. Mayor Alderman H. J. Hine, to commemorate the Queen's Coronation in 1953, presented these formal gardens to the town.

Park Walk, c. 1900. This is the west end of the park, at the top of Stoney Path. A map of 1886 shows a bandstand at the centre of the walk. This could possibly be the bandstand to the right of this scene, behind the tree.

Park Walk, looking down to St James, c. 1900. The Two Brewers public house is to the right at the bottom of the hill. It is interesting to note the lack of houses in the background along Layton Lane, up to Hawksdene and along Frenchmill Lane. An enterprising landlord of the Two Brewers realised the potential of the view and painted the words: 'Ye Olde Two Brewers' on the roof of the pub. This can still be seen today.

Park Walk, *c.* 1910. This Russian cannon, a relic of the Crimean war, stood at the end of Abbey Walk, outside the hospital. It was captured at the siege of Sevastopol in 1855.

Park Walk, *c.* 1925. The cannon was positioned in different places along the park over the years.

Park Walk, *c.* 1930. The cannon from Sevastopol was not the only artillery piece that ended up in Shaftesbury. Both these guns were taken away as scrap metal, in early 1940, to be melted down to help the war effort. As the large Russian cannon was being dragged up Abbey Walk, a massive hole opened up in the ground, but no one appeared to have explored it and it was filled in again.

Abbey Ruins, *c.* 1960. In 888, King Alfred commissioned the building of the Abbey and it was said he installed his daughter, Ethelgyva, as the first Abbess. This Benedictine order remained here for 651 years until the Dissolution in 1539, when the Abbey was taken down. Over a period of time a lot of the stone was plundered and used to build houses around the town.

Abbey Ruins, 1931. The Abbey had many royal connections. King Edward came to the throne in 975, at the age of thirteen. Three years later he was dead. The story goes that King Edward was hunting in Wareham Forest and, knowing that his half brother was at Corfe Castle, decided to ride to see him. Legend has it that his stepmother stabbed him while he was on his horse, which bolted and dragged his body for several miles. She had his body hidden in a well in the house of a blind woman who, on touching his body, regained her sight. This phenomenon was followed by many more stories of miraculous cures. King Edward's body was buried at Wareham but, a year later in 979, pilgrims carried it to the Abbey, where he was buried. The fame of King Edward grew with the number of cures effected there and he became known as St Edward King and Martyr. His bones were hidden at the dissolution of the Abbey and were discovered in 1931 during excavations. This is the casket that, supposedly, contained the bones.

Abbey Ruins, 1936. Church Union pilgrimage to the shrine of St Edward King and Martyr, 1936: the first pilgrimage following a lapse of 400 years.

Abbey Ruins, *c.* 1930. Forty-one burial sites have been found in the Abbey grounds. This is a fourteenth-century internment: the preservation of the bones, lying for so long in the ground, is remarkable.

Westminster Memorial Hospital, *c.* 1920. The widow of the Marquis of Westminster gave the hospital to the town in 1871. It is pictured here before the building of any of the extensions it has received over the years. In the early days of the hospital, patients were only allowed visitors on Thursdays and Sundays and, if they were well enough, had to help clean the wards.

Westminster Memorial Hospital, c. 1925. Up until 1948, when the National Health Service was introduced, the hospital was financed with donations, patient fees and carnival collections. A sign on the wall behind the lamp-post is asking for such contributions. Below the sign is a collection box.

Westminster Memorial Hospital, c. 1940. New wards, on the left, have been added. Further extensions were built in later years to increase the size of the hospital to what it is today.

The Infant School, *c.* 1930. This was built in 1871. This is the school fictionalized in Thomas Hardy's *Jude the Obscure*, when his heroine, Sue Brideshead, comes to teach here following her marriage. Sadly, only part of the original building remains today and it is now a private house.

Ox House, Bimport Street, *c.* 1900. Some parts of this building date back to the sixteenth century. This is the 'Old Grove Place' in Thomas Hardy's *Jude the Obscure*. It was also a public house, in the seventeenth and eighteenth centuries, called the Ox Inn.

47

Pine Walk, looking up towards Park Walk, *c.* 1900. Pine Walk has not altered much since this photograph was taken. It is a splendid place to walk nowadays – but how much more tranquil it must have been then without the noise of traffic!

Pine Walk, *c.* 1900. This young boy has stopped to pose near the entrance onto St John's Hill.

Pine Walk, *c.* 1900. Behind the trees can be seen some of the houses in Love Lane. At the time there were not many buildings there, the western end consisting of allotment gardens.

STONEY PATH

Stoney Path, *c.* 1900. A group of young children pause in their play, unaware of the wonderful addition they make to this photograph.

Three
Gold Hill and St James

Gold Hill, *c.* 1930. This is one of the most photographed and picturesque streets in England. The cottages cling to each other down the hill. It used to be said that if one house were to be removed, the whole lot would tumble down. On the other side are the massive, buttressed walls of the Old Abbey. These buildings beautifully frame the view of the hills beyond. John Schlesinger used this scene to great effect in his film interpretation of Thomas Hardy's *Far from the Madding Crowd*.

St Peter's church, *c.* 1920. A young girl sits on the steps of the old entrance into the church. Behind the church is the Sun and Moon cottage which, at one time, was a public house. A sign can be seen on the wall of the cottage which reads, 'Good lodgings for travellers provided'.

Gold Hill, *c.* 1895. This is a rare photograph. The last house at the top of the hill was the old Lamb Inn, which was both a public house and, later, a poorhouse. It was demolished at the turn of the century.

Gold Hill, *c*. 1900. The old Lamb Inn has been demolished and a new building stands in its place. Although Gold Hill is very picturesque, it was anything but affluent. Large, poor families occupied the cottages and there were numerous doss-houses.

Gold Hill, Shaftesbury

Gold Hill, 1973. Gold Hill was used for a forty-five second commercial for Hovis, which depicted a young boy on a bicycle delivering bread. Anyone who knows Gold Hill will realise that to ride a bicycle down those cobbles is not an easy thing to do!

Gold Hill, c. 1980. In 1982, Hovis found the young boy from the advertisement and brought him back to Shaftesbury in order to present a £10,000 cheque towards the restoration of the cobbles. The loaf in the picture was used as a collection box.

St James, c. 1930. St James' School can be seen on the right at the front of this scene. With the demise of so many of Shaftesbury's schools, it's good to see this establishment is still open today. Further up the street can be seen the open space where Ratcliff's Gardens now stand.

St James, from the top of St James' church, c. 1900. In the centre is the roof of the Fox and Hounds public house, on the corner of Tanyard Lane, which is being re-thatched. The row of nine cottages on the right, further up the street, was called Poor Yard. The author's grandmother, Annie Hayter (née Short), lived in one of these very tiny cottages along with her twelve brothers and sisters.

St James, c. 1950. A clean-up operation is in progress after a painter using a blowtorch accidentally set fire to a house. The fire spread rapidly through this row of cottages with devastating effect.

Shaftesbury's Fire Engine from 1744. This marvellous, old, hand-pulled fire engine would have been of limited use in the fire of the previous photograph! It was used for over 100 years and was housed in one of the lock-up stores behind the Town Hall. A bell on the end of the building was rung to summon the water carriers as well as any of the townspeople who volunteered to help. The engine is now in Shaftesbury's museum.

St James, from the top of St James' church, *c.* 1900. The old rectory stands at the front of this view up St John's Hill. A few houses can be seen along Laundry Lane. Notice the lack of houses on both sides of St John's Hill, when compared with today.

St John's Hill, *c.* 1920.

St Johns Hill, *c.* 1950. Houses have now been built down the hill but the road is still much narrower than it is today.

St James Common, looking towards Shaftesbury, *c.* 1900. Holy Trinity church can be seen on the horizon

Four

Around the Town

Shaftesbury from the air, *c.* 1930. This is looking down Bimport Street. Holy Trinity church can be seen at the front. The tight cluster of houses and the cattle market are where the Bell Street car park is today.

Shaftesbury from the air, *c.* 1940. This is looking up Salisbury Street towards the town. Some new housing has appeared in Boundary Lane. A row of trees and a field occupy the space where the football club and Coppice Street car park are now.

Parsons Pool, *c.* 1910. At the end of Bell Street, the railings of the old cattle market can just be seen. This photograph must have been taken after 1907, because the Weslyan chapel has been rebuilt.

Parsons Pool, *c.* 1920. Mr Stretch, grocer and confectioner, has his shop at the corner of Parsons Pool. The shop window is immaculately laid out with a display of tins and boxes. His delivery vans are parked outside.

Victoria Street, *c.* 1920. The row of houses on the right, with the exception of the last house which has gone and been replaced with a public garden, looks much the same today. The building at the end, on the corner of Bleke Street, with the tall chimney, was Farris' Belle Vue Ironworks. This was Shaftesbury's largest industry at the time, employing up to eighty men.

Bell Street, looking up towards Barton Hill, c. 1910. The cottages on the left have a marvellous design worked into the brickwork behind the lamp-post. Bell Street contains some of the oldest buildings in Shaftesbury.

Bimport Street, facing towards Holy Trinity church, *c.* 1900. The young boy is wearing a black armband. He may be in mourning for one of his relatives or, possibly, for the death of Queen Victoria in 1901.

Bimport Street, *c.* 1920. Children playing safely in the street with their dogs, without the dangers of traffic. In the sale of 1919, the cottages on the right were sold for between £400 and £500 per pair.

The Savoy cinema, Bimport Street, c. 1950. This out-of-character building was built in the 1930s and demolished in the 1980s. It was an extraordinary construction in this setting, having used part of an old barn, which previously stood on this site, as one of its walls. The flats that stand here today are called Savoy Court.

Castle Hill, c. 1950. This was a well-used recreation area in the 1950s and 1960s. A game of cricket is in progress in the foreground. The two shelters, which have since been removed, are clearly visible behind the players.

Enmore Green, *c.* 1920. The Methodist church dominates the centre of this landscape.

Enmore Green, from Castle Hill, across the Blackmore Vale, *c.* 1930. The only changes that have taken place here, since this photograph was taken, is the addition of a few more houses.

Enmore Green, *c.* 1910. The Fountain Inn is in the centre on the right. The Inn got its name because Enmore Green was once the source of supply for Shaftesbury's water, which was taken up Tout Hill on the backs of horses and donkeys.

Holy Trinity church, *c.* 1900. This was Shaftesbury's main church until its deconsecration in 1974. It is now a day centre and offices for various local organisations. Fortunately, the fine avenue of Lime trees has survived.

Holy Trinity interior, *c*. 1940. The inside of the church as it originally was. It has now been partitioned off into various rooms.

Holy Trinity, 1905. The Revd F. Ehluers, rector of the church.

Holy Trinity, 1952. On Sunday 6 July, during a violent thunderstorm, the capping on one of the pinnacles of the tower was struck by lightning. Fortunately, this occurred at 6 am, before the early morning service.

Holy Trinity, 1952. The capping, where it landed on the path below, just outside the main entrance.

Tout Hill, *c.* 1930. The remains of the old Abbey wall, which ran up Tout Hill across Bimport (where there was possibly a gate), can be seen on the left. This met up with the wall running up Gold Hill. Of the five turnpike roads, which converged on Shaftesbury in the eighteenth and nineteenth centuries, Tout Hill was the steepest. Extra horses were needed to pull the coaches up the hill, where they would come to rest in the courtyard of the Grosvenor Hotel – then called the Red Lion. These coaches had grand names such as *Quicksilver* and *The Phoenix*.

Tout Hill, *c.* 1915. The house on the right, now the Ship Inn, was originally a doctor's surgery in the early part of this century.

Post Office workers, *c.* 1930. The post office in the Commons closed before 1930 and was relocated to a building opposite the Ship Inn. This site is now part of the Bell Street car park. The workers are, from left to right, back row: Fred Rideout, Mr Payne, -?-, Jack Brockway, Mr Ambrose. Middle row: -?-, Stan Parsons, Albert Foot, Harry White, Harry Willis, Jack Imber, -?-, -?-, -?-, Harry London. Front row: -?-, Herbert Watts, Frank Buckland, -?-, the postmaster (name unknown), Bill Ware, -?-, Miss Wright.

New Road/Bleke Street, *c.* 1910. New Road was built in the nineteenth century to provide an easier, more gradual ascent into the town. A drinking fountain, which is still there today although now set back against the wall, was installed for refreshment after ascending the hill from Gillingham and Motcombe.

Bleke Street, *c.* 1900. A group of men stand outside the entrance to the old cattle market. The rings used to tie up the cattle can still be seen on one of the remaining old walls of the cattle market. The building on the left is now Sunridge Hotel.

The Beeches, *c.* 1920. Looking up from New Road, the houses at the end of Haimes Lane can just be seen through the avenue of trees.

The Beeches, *c.* 1930.

Ivy Cross, *c.* 1910. The houses in this scene look very similar today. The nearest four houses were built in 1899, the others probably slightly earlier. The opposite side of the road (out of this shot) however, is very different today, with the addition of a garage and roundabout.

Dark Lane, *c.* 1920. This is a road that many people may well have never heard of. The top of Dark Lane can be found about twenty yards down the A30 from the Ivy Cross roundabout, on the right. Today it is just a footpath that runs down to the Motcombe road, at the bottom of New Road.

THE CORNER, GILLINGHAM ROAD, SHAFTESBURY

Gillingham Road, *c.* 1920. This is at the bottom of New Road and is also known as Nettlebeds.

The Round House, *c.* 1970. This toll-house stood at the junction of the Salisbury and Blandford roads, near the Half Moon public house. This is approximately where the roundabout is today.

Five

Special Events

Cann, 1910. Mr Tyler was Shaftesbury's leading photographer at the turn of the century. This is one of his photographs of the United Temperance fête at Cannfield Park on 31 August.

St John's Ambulance, 1929. This is probably a recruiting vehicle, just before the setting up of the Shaftesbury St John's Ambulance. The banner on the van shows the first meeting is to be held on 16 October.

St John's Ambulance, c. 1930. The members of Shaftesbury's St John's Ambulance, outside the Town Hall. From left to right, back row: William Stacey, Walter Alner and William Peddle. Second row (left of ambulance): Mr Newton, Jack Wathen, -?-, Mr Franklin, Charlie Parsons, Carol Rutter, -?-, -?- and Billie Brickell; (right of ambulance) William Dennis, Miss Peach, Jim Saunders, William Welch, Jack London and Farley Tucker (ambulance builder). Front row (seated): -?-, Miss King, Mrs Franklin, Mrs Brockway, Miss Evans, Mrs Hillier and Mrs Mayo.

Enmore Green, looking up towards Tout Hill, c. 1920. The Fountain Inn is in the middle of the houses behind the crowd. This parade is heading towards the sight of the war memorial, so it could well be celebrating its unveiling. Whatever the occasion, the crowd are certainly dressed in their Sunday best.

Viking Visit, 1949. King Canute died in Shaftesbury on 12 November 1035. A crew of modern day Danish Vikings rowed from Denmark in a replica of a Viking longboat, *The Huggin*, to celebrate the 1500th anniversary of Hengist and Horsa landing in England. They were invited to Shaftesbury on 4 August 1949, because of its connection with King Canute. The Vikings made a tour of the town and the Abbey ruins. One of the Vikings, complete with winged helmet, can be seen in the centre of the crowd outside Boots.

Viking Visit, 1949. A number of Danes in costume can be seen in the huge crowd outside the Town Hall.

Youth Sunday, May 1950. The Shaftesbury Grammar School Combined Cadet Force, leading a parade.

Youth Sunday, May 1950. The parade has reached Holy Trinity church from Bimport Street. The Girl Guides and Brownie groups are waiting to enter the church for a service.

Grosvenor Hotel, *c.* 1950. A splendid looking carriage has pulled up outside the hotel, giving us a glimpse of the days when this was a main route for coaches from London through to Exeter. The Grosvenor Hotel was the main coaching inn in Shaftesbury.

The post office, *c.* 1950. The coach is now outside the post office, heading up Coppice Street, which was one of the main ways into the town over the last few centuries.

Women's Institute Play, c. 1970. The two women on the right of the picture are Edna Olsen and Bronwyn Kerle.

Building of Shaftesbury Boys' Club, 1970. L.W. Perry and Sons are machine digging the foundations for the building. Christy's Lane and the primary school can be seen in the background. Note the absence of houses in front of the school.

Building of Shaftesbury Boys' Club, 1970. The houses in Coppice Street are just behind the excavation work.

Shaftesbury Boys' Club, *c.* 1971. The entrance of the new clubhouse. From left to right, back row: Shirley Stretch, Ron Panton, Jimmy Olsen, Andrew Watson. Front row: Terry Burr, Pam Jacobs, Rhoda Conduit, Angela Alford, Mary Brooks, Jenny ?. The fashions of the early seventies are clearly evident.

Coronation of King Edward VII, 1902. The tailors shop next to the Wilts and Dorset Bank, in the High Street, is wonderfully decorated with flags and signs.

Funeral of King Edward VII, 1910. This photograph was taken outside the Town Hall. The Shaftesbury Fire Brigade can be seen on the right, passing Harriet Norton's shop.

Coronation of King George V, 1911. A marvellous scene looking from the Town Hall towards the Commons. The Union Jack is flying above the shop of Strange and Sons, bootmakers and leather merchants.

Coronation of King George VI, 1936. This is no. 8, Barton Hill. The occupants won first prize for the decoration of their house. The sign over the door reads 'Long May He Reign'.

Coronation of Queen Elizabeth II, 2 June 1953. Children are queuing up outside Pikes garage and into Park Walk, waiting to collect their free commemorative cups outside the Town Hall.

Coronation of Queen Elizabeth II, 1953. The mayor, Jack Hine, is handing out commemorative cups. To the left is Mr Orman, the town clerk, and to the right is Mrs Cole. Walter Humphries is far right. The girl collecting her cup is Sandra Farris: her brother, Nigel, and sister, Pat, stand behind.

Coronation of Queen Elizabeth II, 1953. The Town Hall is decorated with bunting.

Coronation Day, 1953. One of the many street parties going on all over the country. This particular event is being held in Hawkesdene Lane, in the garden of Mr Lill.

Coronation Day, 1953. Ice creams all round on this fine day! From front to back, left-hand side of the table: Sandra Farris, Pat Farris, Mrs Farris. Right-hand side: Edna Olsen, Phyllis Olsen, Joyce Gatehouse, Mrs Gatehouse, Jennifer Gatehouse and Mr Collier.

Coronation Day, 1953. The men take a pause from the celebrations for a welcome glass of beer. From left to right, back row: Mr Simms, -?-, Mr Collier, Mr James, Mr Lill. Front row: Mr Plumber, Mr Farris and Mr Thorne.

Coronation Day, 1953. An egg and spoon race (or, as in this case, tennis ball and spoon race). The competing ladies are, from left to right: Miss Lavender, -?-, Mrs Collier, Mrs Lill, Mrs Olsen, Mrs Farris, -?-, Mrs Waller, -?-, -?-, Mrs Humphries.

Coronation Day, 1953. From left to right, back row: Mrs Humphries and Mr Humphries. Front row: Mrs Olsen, Mrs Farris, Mrs Gatehouse. The young boy at the front is the author's brother, Jimmy Olsen.

Six
Carnival Memories

Carnival, *c.* 1930. Gus Bealing, a well-known photographer from Shaftesbury, took this picture. Miss Margaret Hussey is the carnival queen. The driver of this splendid looking float, coming down the Commons, has his view completely obscured by flowers.

Carnival, 1937. The crowning of the carnival queen, Edna Olsen (née Hayter).

Carnival, 1937. The queen and her two attendants: Hazel Simms (on the left) and Edna Stretch.

Carnival, 1938. The carnival queen, Betty Davitt. In the second row are Barbara Broomfield
and Pamela Broomfield.

Carnival, c. 1930. Miss D. Taylor, one of the
many carnival collectors over the years. Most
of the funds generated by the event at this
time went to the running of Shaftesbury's
hospital.

Carnival, 1952. The carnival princess enjoying the occasion.

Carnival, 1952. The carnival queen and her attendants.

Carnival, 1953. The carnival princess, Valerie Croxford.

Carnival, 1953. Roger Kenyan in his imaginative costume of a box of Omo washing powder. The girl with the flowers on her dress is Elizabeth Hardy and Jean Humphries is behind her, to the right.

Carnival 1953. Gordon Green, on the right, wins second prize in the 'Boys under Six' category.

Carnival, 1955. The Carnival Queen, Ida Coombs, with her attendants, Audrey Coombs, Patricia Fulcher, Janet Cox, Peggy Ashby, Jennifer Stokes and pageboy, Jimmy Olsen.

Seven
Schooldays

48434. SHAFTESBURY, The Grammar School.

Grammar School, *c.* 1915. The school was built in 1878 for approximately sixty boys, including fifteen boarders. It grew rapidly over the years with many additional buildings being added, including two laboratories in 1899. The town guide of 1905 describes the school as 'giving special attention to boys of a delicate nature on account of its bracing climate and healthy surroundings'.

Grammar School, *c*. 1936. The school had an extensive sports field attached to it, now the site of the new Upper School. Sport, as in every public school, was especially encouraged and those catered for included: rugby, football, cricket and squash. There was even a croquet lawn at the back of the school. This photograph must have been taken after 1935, as this is when the new physics laboratory to the right was added.

Grammar School, First XI Football Team, 1930.

Grammar School Cricket Team, 1932. Although the order in which they appear in this photograph is not known, the members of the team were: R.S. Balhatchet, A.W. Harding, R. Jeeves, M. Wakefield, P. W. Ball, P. Bathurst Brown, R. Russell, C.H. Burrows and N.A. Welch.

Grammar School Old Boys Football Team, 1925/26.

Girls' High School, *c.* 1910. This was originally Grosvenor House Academy for young gentlemen in the eighteenth and nineteenth centuries. It became the Grosvenor High School for girls in the middle of the 1800s. It is now an architect's office and the gardens are part of the car park.

Girls' High School, 1905. A school photograph taken in the gardens. This was also a kindergarten, a fact which accounts for the young boys sat at the front. A note, written on the back of this picture, reveals that it was from a young girl, called Freda, to her mother. It reads, 'I still have my arm in a sling and am likely to for several days'. Freda is obviously the girl on the right of the top row.

Secondary Modern School, 1983. This school was situated in Mampitts Lane. It was built in the 1950s but, with the introduction of comprehensive education, it became surplus to requirements in 1983 and was pulled down. It was also at this time that the Girls' High School closed and the new Upper School was built on the Grammar School's playing fields.

Enmore Green Primary School, c. 1990. This is another of Shaftesbury's disappearing schools. This was closed after 153 years and has now been converted to a private house.

Enmore Green School, *c.* 1905. A school photograph taken just to the left of the school's entrance.

Enmore Green School, *c.* 1990. A celebration by 250 pupils, past and present, was held to mark the closing of the school. This photograph was taken at the moment when 250 balloons were released as a moving tribute to a much-loved school. Mrs Ivy Brickell, in white in the centre, was the oldest ex-pupil present: she had first registered in the infant class in 1901.

Cann Primary School, 1952. Miss Sharratt takes the children for a P.E. lesson in the playground. The houses behind are in St George's Road.

Cann Primary School, 1952. The boys, from left to right, are: Danny Wigg, -?-, -?-, Keith Lear, Jeff Dyer, -?-, Jimmy Olsen, Phillip Clements and -?-. The girls are: Christine Willis (in front), Pat Farris (behind on the left), Phyllis Olsen (far right). The head teacher, Mrs Edwards, is just to the right of the steps.

Cann School, *c.* 1962. From left to right, back row: Linda Crocker, Rhoda Conduit, Eric Olsen, Stephen Witt, -?-, Malcolm Ransome. Middle row: Diane Alford, Elvin Booth, Barry Booth, Nicky Burr, Andrew Watson, -?-. Front row: -?-, Gordon Yeatman, Terry Burr, Sandra Downs, Robert Downs, Maureen Downs and Mary Brookes.

Cann School, *c.* 1964. From left to right, back row: Nigel Collis, Bill James, -?-, Malcolm Ransome, Nicky Burr, Robert Downs, Eric Olsen, Stephen Witt, Ian Redwood, Martin Dyer. Middle row: ? Dobbs, -?-, Rhoda Conduit, Susan Dobbs, Lesley Alford, Anne Hayes, Gillian Toogood, Stuart Maskell, Hayden Booth, -?-, -?-. Front row: Rachael Collis, -?-, -?-, Dianne Toogood, Janet Best, -?-, Margaret Brookes, -?- and -?-.

Eight
Public Houses

The Mitre Inn, *c.* 1945. This photograph was taken not long after the end of the Second World War: note the air raid siren on the roof of the Town Hall. Bed and breakfast at this time was 14s 6d a night. Longer-term accommodation, including an evening meal, was seven and a half guineas per week.

The Knowles Arms, *c.* 1915. Over the centuries, Shaftesbury has been renowned for its brewing and public houses. Thomas Hardy once commented that 'Shaftesbury was a place where beer was more plentiful than water, and where there were more wanton women than honest wives and maids'. The reason for the profusion of beer was the problematic water supply, as Shaftesbury is on top of a hill, and the sheer number of inns and brewhouses. The Knowles Arms and the Spiller's Almshouse, to its right, were both pulled down in the late 1970s.

The Grosvenor Hotel, *c.* 1890. Seen here with horse-drawn coaches waiting outside, this coaching inn is one of the oldest public houses in Shaftesbury. It was called the Red Lion up until 1826. These coaches were used to carry passengers to and from Semley Station. The journey to the station was quick but, because of the steepness of Semley Hollow, it was nearly as quick to walk on the return journey back to Shaftesbury!

The Grosvenor Hotel, *c.* 1920. Transport has progressed and these fine omnibuses, belonging to th hotel, have replaced the horse-drawn carriages. They charged 1/- each way and this was said to be one of the dearest rides in the country. To the right of the Grosvenor was the Star public house, which became the Grosvenor Tap and is now part of the hotel.

The Grosvenor Hotel, *c.* 1930. The hotel building is an imposing sight that dominates the Commons.

The Ship Hotel, *c.* 1900. This public house stood opposite Bimport Street and is not to be confused with the present day Ship, which is at the top of Tout Hill. Just behind the Ship Hotel can be seen the Rose and Crown. It is worth noting the skilful display in the shop window of Strange Brothers, on the corner of Bimport Street.

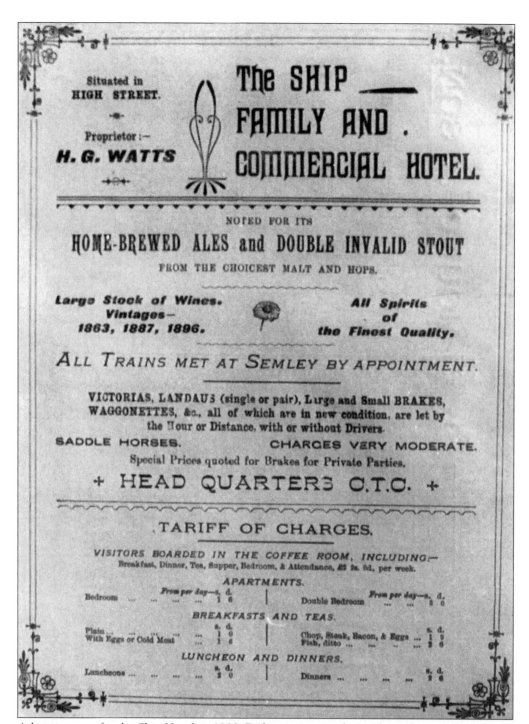

Advertisement for the Ship Hotel, *c.* 1900. Bedrooms were only 1s 6d a night at this time. Like many pubs at the turn of the century, The Ship brewed its own beer, including 'Double Invalid Stout'. It was also the headquarters of the Cyclist Touring Club, a very popular pastime at the turn of the century.

Sketch of the Royal Chase Hotel, *c.* 1925. This was originally a private residence called Belmont House. Just before the turn of the century, it was inhabited by a group of Benedictine monks and later sold to an order called 'The Sons of Mary Immaculate' to train French Roman Catholic priests. It was sold in 1922 and became the Royal Chase Hotel.

Ye Olde Two Brewers, *c.* 1900. The dray stands outside, although whether it was delivering beer or collecting beer for delivery to another pub is impossible to say. The Hand in Hand public house was a little further down St James on the right. Centuries before there had also been the White Hart and The Ben of Leather, which was frequented by the workers of the tanneries in St James.

108

The Two Brewers, *c.* 1900. From the appearance of the trees on Park Walk above, I think this photograph was probably taken in the spring. A small dog is looking at the photographer as he takes this picture.

The Two Brewers, *c.* 1900. Similar to the last scene, but now it is summer, as the roses on the arches are in full bloom. The dog seems to be enjoying the sunshine.

The Fox and Hounds, *c.* 1900. A chimney sweep is stood on the corner of Tanyard Lane. Children from all over St James have come to join in this photograph. The author's grandmother, Annie Hayter (née Short), who would have been about five or six at this time, used to live almost opposite this pub – perhaps she is one of these children?

The Fox and Hounds, looking down towards St James' church, *c.* 1900. This public house was closed in the fifties and is now a private home.

Nine
In the Snow

Cann School, 1908. Anyone who knows Shaftesbury will know that it has its own unique climate. Shaftesbury will always get more than its fair share of snow because of its exposed height. This is the record-breaking snowstorm of 25 April 1908. Cann School is on the left. Past the school is Belmont House, now the Royal Chase Hotel. Through the trees can be seen Cann House, which was later demolished: the roundabout now stands in its place.

Butts Knap, *c.* 1940. The snow-covered trees frame the Grammar School.

Butts Knap, *c.* 1950. This was obviously taken after a heavy snowfall. Before the roundabout and the new road outside the Royal Chase Hotel was built, the main A350 road to Blandford was to the right of the war memorial.

Hawkesdene, *c.* 1950. Christmas Day in Hawkesdene Lane: was this the trail left by Santa and his reindeers?

Salisbury Street, *c.* 1920. A woman on horseback features in this snowscene. The row of small cottages, in the centre to the right, have since been demolished.

Hawkesdene Farm, 1950. This bus was heading for Okeford Fitzpaine. Heavy snow, drifting against the walls outside Clarke's Farm, forced the driver to abandon it.

Hawkesdene Farm, 1950. Farm workers are clearing a path. The farm, including the milking parlour directly behind the tree on the left, has now been converted into houses.

Ten
View of the Villages

Semley Hollow, *c.* 1900. As most Shastonians will know, all the roads that lead into the town are very steep! Horse-drawn coaches from the Grosvenor and Ship Hotels used to bring passengers from Semley station up the hollow.

Wincombe Farm, *c.* 1900. A lady in her pony and trap is waiting outside the farm. In stark contrast, a farm labourer stands behind with his horse and cart.

Cann Hill, *c.* 1925. A lorry struggles up the steep hill from Shaftesbury.

Cann, *c.* 1930. A view of Cann taken from the top of Melbury Hill. Holy Trinity church can just be seen on the horizon to the left.

Cann, *c.* 1900. A steam engine accident at Cann. A vehicle belonging Fred Sharp and Sons, steam haulage contractors of Blandford, was loaded with bricks when it turned over outside the premises of Mr Short the carpenter.

Melbury Hill, *c.* 1900. This is from the top of Zig Zag, looking towards Melbury Hill.

Melbury Hill, *c.* 1910.

Melbury Abbas, *c.* 1900. At the bottom of Spread Eagle Hill, outside the Spread Eagle Inn, a woman is enjoying the fine weather with her baby. Shaftesbury can just be seen in the distance.

Coombe House, *c.* 1915. This house was built in 1886 for Mark Hanbury Beaufoy, a vinegar manufacturer from Bermondsey.

Coombe House, *c.* 1930. Like many large country houses in the area, Coombe House was sold and became a hotel in the 1930s.

St Mary's Convent, *c.* 1950. From being a hotel and, at the end of the Second World War, a convalescent home for injured soldiers, Coombe House was sold and turned into St Mary's Convent and School – which it still is today.

Coombe House Lodge, *c.* 1950. The Lodge House on the main Salisbury road, at the end of the drive to Coombe House, was a tearoom at this time.

Motcombe House, *c.* 1900. This private house was built in 1894 on the site of a much older residence. It was the home of Lord Stalbridge, who owned much of Shaftesbury until 1919. The house is now Port Regis School.

Motcombe church, *c.* 1920. This church was rebuilt in 1846. To the left of the church is the school, built in 1874. Unlike many small village schools it is still open today.

MOTCOMBE POST OFFICE.

Motcombe Post Office, *c.* 1920. The post office is the thatched building behind the trees. The post mistress in the twenties was a Mrs Stainer. The Laurels and Stone Cottage are to the right, on the road up to Shaftesbury.

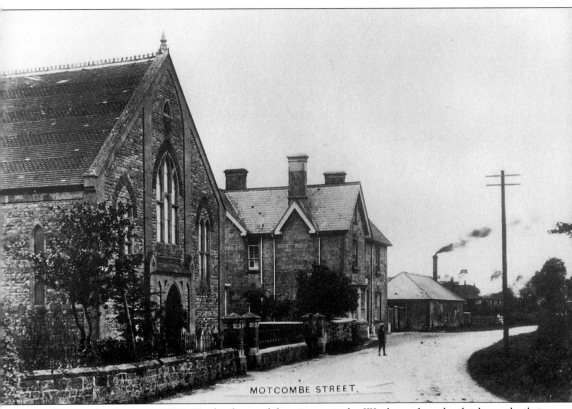

MOTCOMBE STREET.

Motcombe Street, *c*. 1910. To the front of the picture is the Weslyan chapel, which was built in 1870. Adjacent to this is the Royal Oak public house, although this bears no sign. The chimney of Prideaux's slaughterhouse, which was also a dairy at this time, can be seen behind the Royal Oak. Prideaux's was the first business to produce powdered baby milk. It is now called Case and Sons.

Motcombe Memorial Hall, *c.* 1960. This hall was built in memory of Lord Stalbridge.

Ashmore, *c.* 1930. The old school looking across to Pond House. North Farm is to the left.

Ashmore, *c*. 1900. This picturesque village, 800 feet above sea level, is the highest in Dorset. The village pond, or mere – which is where the original name Ashmere came from, is one of the deepest on the chalk cliffs.

Ashmore, looking down the High Street towards the village pond, *c.* 1930. The distinctive Weslyan chapel, built in 1855, is on the right. The houses on the left are older and date from 1837.

Ashmore, *c.* 1930. The New House, seen here looking down the drive on the outskirts of the village, has changed little since it was built.

Compton Abbas, *c.* 1920. The village shop was closed only a few years ago, when the owner, Mr Ellingham, retired. His father, who is probably the man in this photograph, originally ran it. The sign on the side of the shop can still just be seen, although this may soon change as the frontage is being renovated. The arched front window has only recently been bricked up. The building behind dates from the seventeenth century and is now Milestones Tearooms. The village church of St Mary's was built in 1867, using some of the stone from the original church.